The
Solar
Cat
Book

The Solar Cat Book

Ten Speed Press
Berkeley, California

Illustrations:
Hildy Paige Burns

By Jim Augustyn

Notice

This book was prepared as work sponsored by the American Section of the International Solar Cat Society (AS/ISCS). Neither the author, the publisher, nor the AS/ISCS make any warranty, expressed or implied, or accept any responsibility for the accuracy or usefulness of any information, apparatus, product or process disclosed, or represent that its use would not infringe privately on the rights or well-being of cats, non-cats, or people.

Ten Speed Press
P.O. Box 7123
Berkeley, California 94707

Thanks

To Bill, Steve, Alana, Priscilla, Carol, Margaurite, Penny, Marshal, Tom, Jerry, Mike, Jack, Kathy, Juanita, Sylvia, Tony, Judy, Bruce, Chip, Max, Murray, Michael, Nancy, Lewis, Phil, and certainly George for many fine suggestions and valuable support.

Extra Special Thanks

To Elizabeth and Hildy for being uncommonly wonderful.

Super Extra Special Furry Thanks

To Mouse, Parsley, Emily, and Ernie, may he purr in peace.

Text for illustration on page 9 from "WE'VE ONLY JUST BEGUN" © 1970, Irving Music, Inc. (BMI) All Rights Reserved. Used With Permission

Lyrics: Paul Williams
Music: Roger Nichols

Library of Congress Card Catalog Number LC 79-8515

To

my most wonderful gray striped friend

Table of Contents

Preface

The concept of a solar cat has a firm basis in reality, familiar to all who know cats. Throughout this book, such reality is mixed with fantasy, requiring the reader to continually distinguish between the two. This process will hopefully promote thought and learning, for as a wise old cat once said: "To learn, it helps to think."

Chapter One

CATS AND THE SUN

HISTORY

Cats love the sun. They have been closely associated with it since time began.

Cats associating with the sun when time began.

Some think that cats invented the sun. Modern science has been unable to prove this theory. Then again, modern science has been just as unable to explain gravity.

Cat inventing the sun.

If cats can prove they invented the sun, some fear those little furry beasts may claim patent rights and impose a stiff tariff on human solar use. If cats try to impose such a tariff they will undoubtedly run into great resistance as most courts and juries are packed with people or at least non-cats. Furthermore, cats are notoriously poor lawyers and have historically failed in such legal crusades.

It is well known that cats were worshipped in ancient Egypt. No doubt the Egyptians recognized how perfectly cats interact with their environment and glorified them appropriately. In ancient Egyptian art the goddess Bast represented the life-giving heat of the sun and was portrayed with the head of a cat. Quite obviously the Egyptians recognized the close connection between cats and the sun.

This "Egyptian Period" witnessed tremendous growth of solar knowledge by cats. During this period cats discovered thermal mass. (Thermal mass is anything that holds heat and especially things which hold a lot of heat.)

Cat discovering how the overwhelming thermal mass or heat storage capacity of the pyramids provides unchanging cool relief from the scorching desert environment.

Even after the decline of Egypt, cats continued to advance in their ability to use the sun, though at times their progress was slow. They traveled by boat to Europe where their solar research activity was severely hampered with the onset of cat-hating religious cults of the Middle Ages. Cruel and arrogant humans forced cats to stay outside where they became experts at chasing mice and rats for survival and entertainment. Although European winters were very cold, cats had by then learned how to use the sun to stay warm, and thus survived this era of persecution. By the early Eighteenth century cats had regained human favor, having eliminated the rats who carried the Black Plague throughout Europe.

At the onset of the industrial revolution cats were much more highly regarded, but with cheap and plentiful coal it seemed hardly worth the effort to study such a seemingly weak energy source as cats using the sun. Being basically messy, people preferred filthy coal to self-cleaning solar cats.

This century has seen people shift from coal to oil as their primary energy source. This change from messiness to sliminess has long been viewed as a natural progression to be followed by a gradual shift to nuclear power.

Unfortunately (or fortunately), nuclear energy cannot be developed as quickly as once thought. Concern for human health and welfare will not permit the rapid growth of nuclear power without extreme caution.

A great shift to energy sources that are renewable in the short term (primarily solar energy) has now begun. With centuries of solar experience behind them, cats are certain to play an important role in this "Great Solar Transition."

Cat playing an important role in the "Great Solar Transition."

THE STATE OF THE ART

Because of their long association with, and study of the sun, cats have an overwhelming advantage over people in the solar field. The future will undoubtedly witness a narrowing of this gap as people become increasingly aware of the potential of solar energy, and devise ever more ingenious ways of using it to their own advantage.

SOLAR KNOWLEDGE COMPARISON*

CATS' SOLAR KNOWLEDGE

PEOPLES' SOLAR KNOWLEDGE

WHERE EACH FIGURE REPRESENTS A WHOLE LOT OF SOLAR KNOWLEDGE

*AS OF JULY 29, 1979

AND ⇨  1 = 100

Certainly, humans are reluctant to admit that cats know more about solar utilization than they do. At times it seems that people refuse to see even the most obvious. The most common example of this involves cats' affinity for sunlight on chilly afternoons. Generations of study have led cats to the astute conclusion that when cold, it makes perfect sense to expose one's fur to the sun.

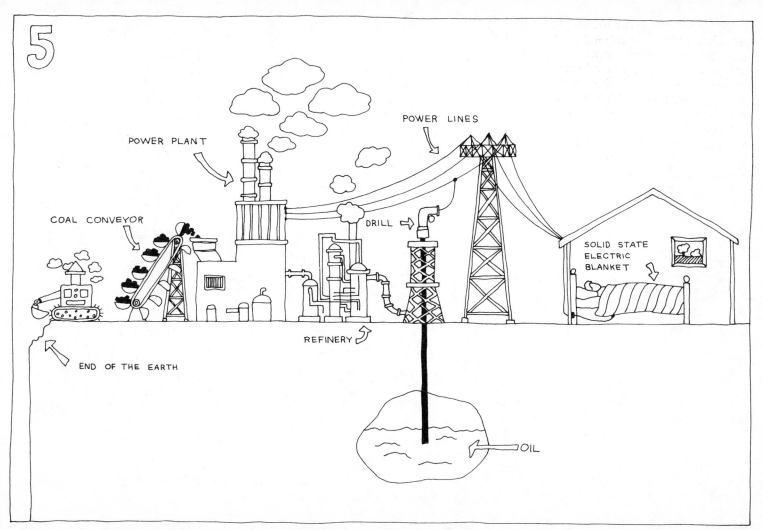

5

POWER PLANT

POWER LINES

COAL CONVEYOR

DRILL

SOLID STATE
ELECTRIC
BLANKET

END OF THE EARTH

REFINERY

OIL

Today, cats can be seen routinely using the sun to meet their energy needs. How common is the sight of a cat curled up in a patch of sunlight? A good guess would be 50 million times a day in the United States alone! This is a good guess because there are about 25 million cats in the U.S., and if on average, each cat is seen twice per day, 50 million daily sightings result.

Two sightings of a cat in a patch of sunlight.

Cats not only use the sun in their everyday lives, they also work hard to improve and perfect their present methods of solar utilization. At times, however, it is not so obvious that cats are involved in solar research and development. Their well-known fondness for going outside in the dark is a prime example of this. Common folklore has it that cats can see in the dark and can therefore hunt well at night. Naturally, this has never been proven since people can't see in the dark to tell what cats are doing out there. Recent evidence has shown that cats can't see at all without light, and what they are really after is to find out where the sun went so they can warm up.

Imagined view of a cat in the dark looking for the sun.

Bird chasing is another well-known facet of cat behavior that has been mistakenly attributed to simple "animal instinct." Their real motive in such pursuit is to learn how birds fly through capture and thorough inspection. Once cats learn how birds fly, they can then get closer to the sun on very cold days.

Flying cat getting closer to the sun.

It is simple to see how cats get warm by exposure to sunlight: when it hits them, they heat up! Of almost equal importance are ways they avoid the sun and the reasons they do this. Obviously, the primary reason cats avoid the sun is to stay cool.

One way cats avoid the sun on hot days is by crawling into paper bags. This displays their skillful use of appropriate technology.

Cat staying cool by being inside a paper bag which happens to be open in the middle of the desert.

21

Another important reason that cats sometimes seek shade is because they are afraid that their suntans will blister if they stay out too long.

Sometimes cats are involved in solar research and development activities when they appear to be just standing around. Many of their research projects deal with such subtle forces that people can barely conceive the true purpose of such apparently ordinary behavior.

Cat absorbing straight, squiggly and dashed heat from the sun while appearing to be just standing around.

The following chapters describe much of what cats have done in the fields of solar thermal and solar electric systems development, with frequent comparison to peoples' efforts.

Because of their vital importance to cat and energy enthusiasts, sections dealing with the economics, selection, training, operation, and maintenance of solar cats have also been included.

Though people have much to learn about solar energy, with cats to guide them, they are assured of eventual success.

Chapter Two

SOLAR THERMAL CATS

Solar thermal cats convert sunlight into heat, and are similar in many ways to peoples' solar thermal systems.

This chapter describes their basic types and component parts offering frequent comparison to peoples' systems.

Passive cat.

PASSIVE CATS AND ACTIVE CATS

There are two kinds of solar thermal cats: passive cats and active cats.

Passive cats sit around all day, often on windowsills, absorbing sun and later letting it go. They hardly do anything except to occasionally go to their food or water dish, or perhaps to their litter box.

Active cat—Mode 1.

Active cats, on the other hand, get up and go after the sun, be it on a garage roof, or on the back fence. They then bring it back inside where it will do some good. All this running around makes active cats much bigger eaters than passive cats, so active cats generally cost more to own and operate.

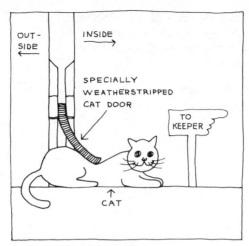

Active cat—Mode 2.

Solar thermal systems designed by people are much the same but are unable to change from active to passive (or vice versa) as cats often do.[1]

Active cat—Mode 3.

[1]The most notable distinction between peoples' passive and active systems is that their active systems need electricity to work while their passive systems do not.

To fully appreciate the functional simplicity of solar thermal cats it is useful to first study the component parts of peoples' systems. Whether passive or active, peoples' systems have four basic parts: collector, storage, heat transfer mechanism, and control.

Collector

All solar thermal systems collect energy during the day, heating the home or office as necessary. In passive systems, collectors take the form of windows, skylights, and greenhouses. In active systems common flat plate collectors are used.

Storage

Once daytime heating needs are met, additional energy is stored for use at night. Such storage can be in tanks of water, piles of rock or dirt, or almost anything else that can hold heat. In passive systems, heat storage often occurs in the building structure itself, as in concrete floors, walls, or furniture.

Heat Transfer Mechanism

In addition to collectors and storage, solar thermal systems must have some way to transfer heat from the collector to the point of use. In active systems, pumps, fans, and a "heat transfer fluid" are used. In passive designs, the heat flows all by itself, such as when warm air rises or heat flows through a wall.

Control

In active systems, preprogrammed electronic controls tell pumps and fans when to run in order to collect, store and distribute energy. In passive systems this control function occurs automatically, though it is sometimes necessary for a person to open and close curtains or a vent.

With cats, all system functions are combined into a single, nearly flawless component: The Cat. In a solar thermal cat, the cat serves as collector, storage, heat transfer mechanism, as well as system controller. In addition, cats make good use of catabolic heat generation, an aspect entirely missing from peoples' systems.[1]

The following sections describe each of the basic solar thermal system components in greater detail, including cats' use of catabolic heat generation. Many of the similarities and differences between cats' and peoples' systems are also described.

[1]Catabolism is the part of metabolism in which heat is released. Anabolism is the other part.

CHART COMPARING CATS' AND PEOPLES' SOLAR THERMAL SYSTEMS

COMPONENT	SOLAR THERMAL CAT		SOLAR THERMAL SYSTEMS MADE BY PEOPLE	
	ACTIVE	PASSIVE	ACTIVE	PASSIVE
COLLECTOR			FLAT PLATE COLLECTOR	
STORAGE			WATER TANK ROCK BIN	CONCRETE BLOCKS
HEAT TRANSFER MECHANISM			FROM HERE TO THERE PUMP WATER INSIDE	MOTHER NATURE
CONTROL			Alpha Beta Electronics	
CATABOLISM			NOT APPLICABLE	NOT APPLICABLE

CATS AS COLLECTORS

Cats have several inherent features which allow them to function as highly efficient, aesthetic solar collectors. Among these are the "heat trap" characteristic of cat fur, cats' ability to be concentrating, tracking, or fixed, and their unique self-cleaning characteristic. Peoples' collectors have many of the same features but are not usually self-cleaning.

Heat Trap Fur

Cats' high solar collection efficiency is primarily due to the "heat trap" characteristic of their fur. When cat fur is properly oriented, squiggly heat rays from the sun neatly slip between the fur to strike the cat skin underneath. This occurs regardless of fur color, but is affected by fur length, thickness and straightness.

Since cat fur prevents wind from getting near the heated cat skin, solar heat striking the cat body is trapped, hence the name "heat trap fur."

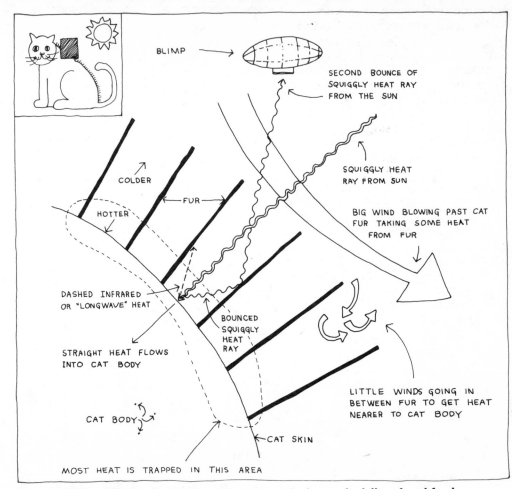

Energy flow diagram illustrating "heat trap" characteristic of cat fur in a properly oriented cat.

Although a few innovative solar collector manufacturers have tried to imitate cat fur's "heat trap" characteristic, most still revert to using glass or plastic "glazings" to reduce heat loss to the air from the collector's absorbing surface.[1]

In most locations a single glazing is adequate for collectors in solar water heating systems. In very cold climates two or even three glazings are needed to reduce heat loss to the surrounding air. Even unglazed collectors (similar to clean-shaven cats) can be effective. They can be used for summertime swimming pool heating since in this case the collector absorber is very nearly the same temperature as the surrounding air, and little heat loss results.

[1]"Glazing" is an architectural term for transparent materials which can be used for windows or flat plate collector covers.

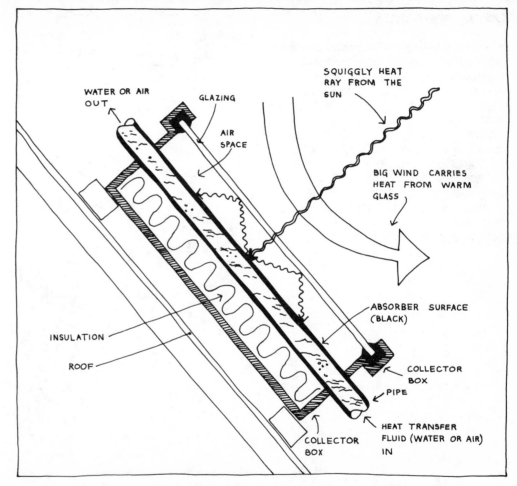

Energy flow diagram illustrating how peoples' collectors utilize a "heat trap" principle of their own without fur.

WATER OR AIR OUT

GLAZING

AIR SPACE

SQUIGGLY HEAT RAY FROM THE SUN

BIG WIND CARRIES HEAT FROM WARM GLASS

ABSORBER SURFACE (BLACK)

INSULATION

ROOF

COLLECTOR BOX

PIPE

HEAT TRANSFER FLUID (WATER OR AIR) IN

COLLECTOR BOX

Catacombs

Since fur orientation is critical to solar cat collection efficiency, methods to ensure proper orientation are extremely important. One promising way of doing this involves combining a cat door with a fur comb so that whenever a cat goes through the door (or "catacomb") its fur is properly arranged. No good method has yet been devised to insure that the cat positions itself properly once it passes through the door but science and technology will surely solve this problem in the end.

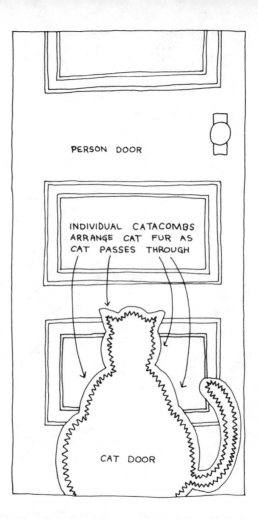

PERSON DOOR

INDIVIDUAL CATACOMBS ARRANGE CAT FUR AS CAT PASSES THROUGH

CAT DOOR

Concentrating Cats

Concentrating cats are not even vaguely similar to peoples' "concentrating" solar collectors, however, they are much more common. Concentrating cats often stare intently for hours at what appears to be nothing. No plausible explanation for this has yet been advanced.

Peoples' concentrating collectors focus or concentrate solar energy onto a small spot or area, just like a magnifying glass in the sun. They usually need to track the sun across the sky although some designs can remain stationary.

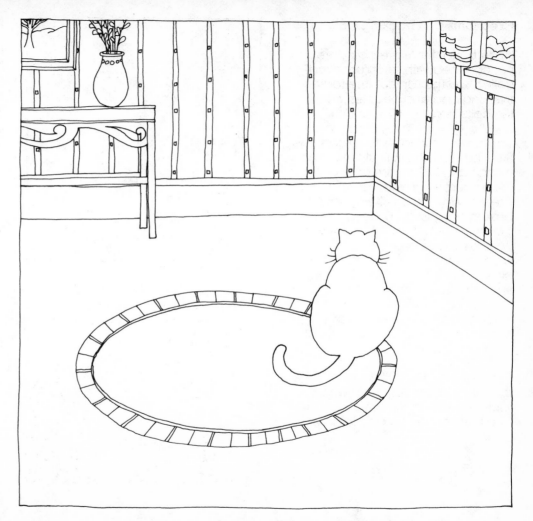

Fixed Cats and Tracking Cats

It is important that fixed cats are not confused with peoples' "fixed" collectors. The same is true for tracking cats and peoples' tracking collectors.

There are two kinds of fixed cats. The first kind are fixed to limit the cat population and in the case of boy cats, to suppress aggressive behavior. The second kind are fixed because broken cats just don't work right.

Peoples' fixed collectors are those which stay in one place and do not change their tilt or orientation to follow the sun across the sky.

Tracking cats are those which sniff out and locate patches of sunlight, birds or mice.

Peoples' tracking collectors change their tilt and orientation to remain faced directly at the sun all day long, and have almost nothing to do with birds or mice.

BROKEN CAT

FIXED CAT

CATS AS THERMAL STORAGE[1]

There are two kinds of thermal storage: "sensible" and "latent." Cats can store heat in both ways, whereas peoples' solar thermal systems usually use only one or the other.

Sensible Heat Storage

Sensible heat storage is "sensible" because it is easily sensed. When something stores sensible heat its temperature increases. Very heavy things store more of it than lightweight things, given the same temperature rise and size of thing. Also, a lightweight object must get much hotter (in temperature) to absorb the same amount of sensible heat as something very heavy.

Cats are so good at storing sensible heat that a fundamental measure of heat energy (the CTU or Cat Thermal Unit) has been named after them.[2]

[1]"Thermal storage" is just a fancy name for heat storage.

[2]CTUs and heat are explained more fully in the Appendix.

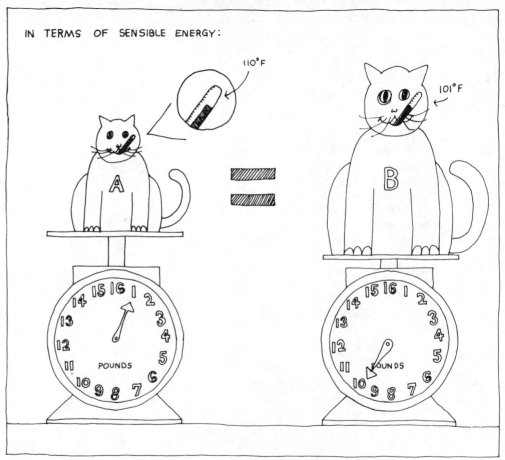

IN TERMS OF SENSIBLE ENERGY:

110°F

101°F

Both cats "A" and "B" started out having temperatures of exactly 100°F and then proceeded to absorb the same amount of heat. Cat "A" became much hotter than cat "B" because cat "B" weighs so much more.

33

Latent Heat Storage

Latent heat storage is not nearly as obvious as the sensible kind. This is because the temperature of the object (or cat) does not change as latent heat is stored or removed.

People are beginning to use latent heat storage in their solar thermal systems by using special materials such as "eutectic" salts. Great amounts of heat can be stored in these materials as they melt at or near room temperature.

With cats, latent heat storage takes place in the formation of purrs. When a cat has been warmed to its normal limit of 102°F excess energy can be stored in what are called "latent purrs."

The exact amount of energy that can be stored in an average purr is unknown. However, some of the softest purrs have warmed the coldest hearts, and it would be folly to ignore such startling effects.

HEART OF ICE

PURR PURR PURR PURR

PUDDLE

Effect of a latent purr on a cold heart.

The Insulating Value of Fur

A common fault of many of peoples' solar thermal systems is that their storage tanks are not well insulated. Sometimes even the best insulating job can be damaged, with great thermal consequences.

This is usually not the case with cats. Cat fur is widely recognized as virtually the ultimate insulating material. It adjusts its insulating value to follow changing seasonal conditions (as in shedding), and grows back to repair shaved or damaged areas.

People may be able to imitate the appearance of cat fur in their own insulating materials. However, it is doubtful that they will ever duplicate the self-adjusting and repairing aspects.

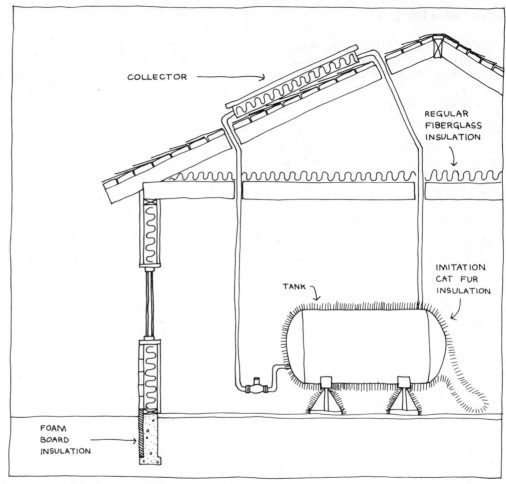

COLLECTOR

REGULAR FIBERGLASS INSULATION

IMITATION CAT FUR INSULATION

TANK

FOAM BOARD INSULATION

Solar water heating system with imitation cat fur insulation on storage tank.

CATS AS HEAT TRANSFER MECHANISM

It is easy to see how cats transport heat. They simply get up and take it wherever they go. People have not yet developed as good a way to move heat around, except perhaps in passive systems where the heat moves around more or less by itself. In active systems, people use liquids or air to transfer heat. Such fluids can leak, turn corrosive or freeze if care is not exercised.

Cat transporting heat.

Freeze Protection

Cats avoid freezing by wearing fur coats and by staying in warm places. Peoples' solar thermal collectors have a much harder time since they spend their entire lives outside without hope of comfort on cold nights. This doesn't pose a great problem except for those collectors which contain liquids which can freeze, possibly damaging the fluid passages.

While freeze protection is a critical issue in peoples' solar systems, fleas protection is of equal concern to solar thermal cats and their owners. Though there is much interest in finding better ways to discourage fleas from bumming around in cat fur, no outstanding method of fleas protection yet exists. Many flea sprays, collars, and tags are available, however, a weekly bath remains the most effective method since fleas enjoy swimming even less than cats.

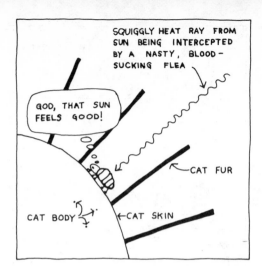

Fleas jumping from bathing cat in "fleas protection" mode.

Corrosion

Cats do not corrode. However, the metallic parts of flat plate and concentrating collectors can, and things must be arranged to keep this from happening. This is usually accomplished by avoiding the use of corrosive materials or by using chemical additives to protect the metal surfaces from corrosion. Another effective method is to use plastic or fiberglass in place of metal.

Corrosion is a dark and murky subject. In most cases it is resolved by experts who figure out what to do and then write instructions to explain how to keep things working the way they should. Unfortunately, not all experts know what they are doing, and even if they do, they are usually poor instruction writers. In any case, it always pays to follow instructions for corrosion protection, since warranties are usually void if you don't, and some experts have been known to be right.

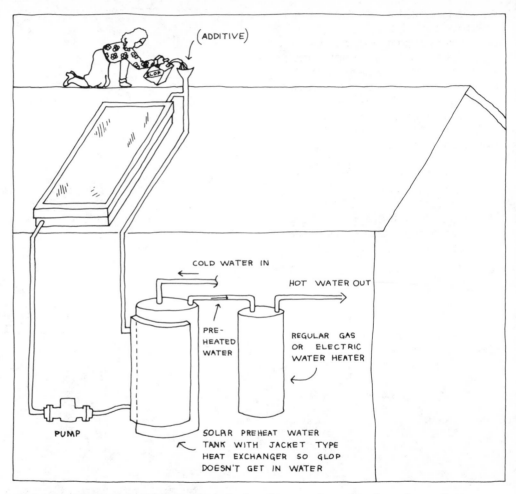

Person adding prescribed amount of anti-corrosive glop to solar system collector "loop" at prescribed interval.

With solar cats, the cat itself is the corrosive agent. Cats take great pleasure in sharpening their claws on common household objects. Prevention of such accelerated wear of internal home surfaces can also be accomplished with the use of additives. Adding a piece of furniture which begs to be scratched is a good additive.

Of course, another method to prevent such damage is to avoid the use of cats, but this is clearly out of the question.

Person adding funny looking scratching post to inside of cat's house to prevent corrosion of other surfaces.

Overheating

One of the worst problems with flat plate or concentrating solar collectors is <u>overheating</u> ("stagnating" in solar jargon). On sunny, hot days when the last thing anyone wants is solar heat, collectors can get extremely hot, sometimes causing heat transfer fluids to turn corrosive or causing other kinds of material failures. This is a greater problem with double glazed and concentrating collectors as their maximum "stagnation temperature" can be well in excess of 400 or even 500°F.

Overheating is never a problem with cats since they move to shady places when the sun gets too hot for them. <u>Overeating</u> is a problem for them though, similar in some ways to alcoholism in people.

CATS AS SYSTEM CONTROLLERS

Cats are always in control. They always know exactly what to do and when to do it. The only possible explanation for this is that they each possess an incredibly sophisticated and complex (although very tiny) control network much like that of a large power plant.

Peoples' solar system controls are not nearly as complicated or socially significant. Active systems use programmed electronic control boxes which are getting smaller all the time. They sense temperatures in various places (principally the collector absorber plate and storage tank) and tell other electric components what to do at the proper time.

Very much enlarged view of cat brain central control room.

CATABOLISM

Catabolism is the part of metabolism in which heat energy is released. The catabolic heat generation rate of a cat depends on its state of activity. For example, a cat at rest discharges catabolic heat at a rate proportional to its weight, approximately according to the following equation:

$$Q = 16.5\,W^{0.75} \quad \text{(Note 1)}$$

Where:

Q = the catabolic heat generation rate in BTUs per hour per cat

W = weight of the cat in pounds

From this equation, the standard 10 pound cat would produce 92.8 BTUs per hour, enough to raise a quart of water from 55 to 100°F.[2]

This is a rather small rate of release, especially when compared to the current total U.S. energy use rate of 2.34 billion BTUs per second. However, even this gargantuan energy demand could be met with the catabolic heat generated by a single, 4.292 million billion pound cat, or only 56,072 100-megaton cats as

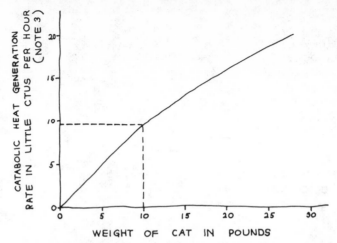

Graph of catabolic heat generation rate versus weight for normal weight cats.

described in Chapter Three. However, it is doubtful that such large cats will ever be developed.

It is certainly possible to breed enough cats of normal weight to satisfy U.S. energy consumption with catabolic heat alone. About 93.2 billion "standard" cats would be adequate for this task. The current U.S. cat population is about 25 million. Luckily, cats are very fast breeders, and like their nuclear counterpart, can theoretically multiply fast enough to meet the challenge.

[1]Reprinted with permission from the 1977 Fundamentals Volume, ASHRAE HANDBOOK & Product Directory.

[2]The "standard cat" is defined in the Appendix.

[3]Both Big and Little CTUs are defined in the Appendix.

Exactly how quickly cats could provide the U.S. with catabolic energy self-sufficiency is easily determined with some simple (though tedious) arithmetic. If the following assumptions are made, approximately 9.3 years would be needed to "fast breed" the necessary number of cats:

1. Everyone tries very hard to help cats breed.

2. The starting cat population is 24 million.

3. Half of all cats are female.

4. Half of all female cats at the commencement of fast breeding are fertile.

5. Each fertile female cat can have two litters of 4 kittens each year.

6. Female cats can litter only between the ages of one and ten.

7. The average life span of all cats is 15 years.

8. All cats are "standard" cats.

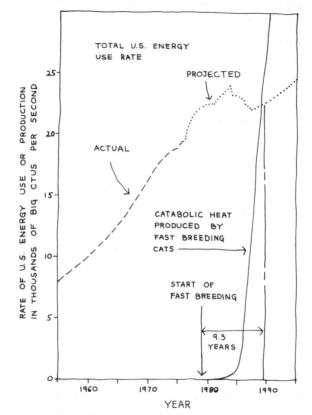

Chart showing how quickly fast breeding cats can solve the energy crisis with catabolic heat generation alone.

APPLICATIONS

The normal function of solar thermal cats is to keep cats warm. However, they can be used by people in a variety of ways. The following examples illustrate a few of the ways solar thermal cats can be applied to human needs.

Residential

Residential applications of solar thermal cats are most practical since cats like to stay close to home. Solar thermal cats are best at space heating but can heat domestic water, swimming pools, and even hot tubs, under the right circumstances.

Peoples' active solar thermal systems are most practical when attempting to supply low temperature heat. Swimming pool heating is therefore most effective, followed by hot tub, domestic water and then building space heating. Passive space heating systems are much more practical than active ones, since they cost less and work much better.

Solar thermal cat providing residential space heat.

Solar thermal cat pre-heating hot tub in residential setting.

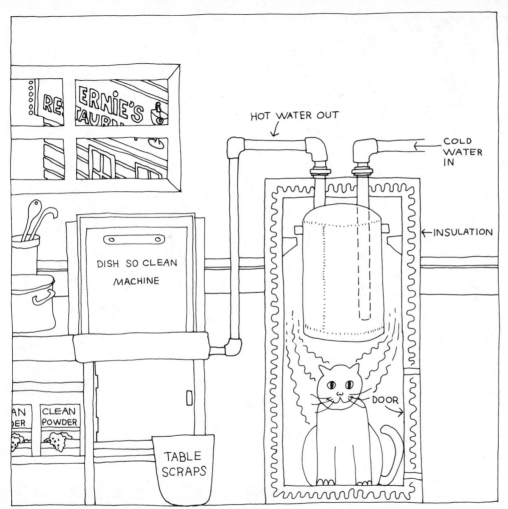

Solar thermal cat heating water in restaurant.

Commercial

Solar thermal cats can also be used in commercial settings, especially in restaurants with tasty table scraps. Peoples' commercial systems have principally been used for water heating in restaurants and hotels, and for swimming pool heating.

Industrial

People have been slow to adopt solar thermal systems in industry. This is partly because the previous low cost of industrial energy fostered great waste. To date, industry has found investment in energy conservation much more profitable than in solar thermal energy production, but is expected to slowly embrace solar technology.

Cats understandably avoid smelly, noisy factories. They can, however, be persuaded to provide people with heat for industrial processes if the rewards are equal to the task.

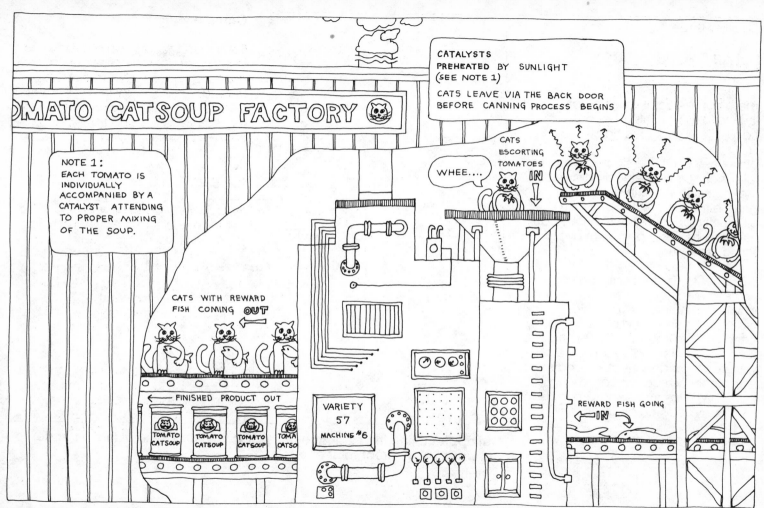

Warm solar thermal cats reduce process heating requirement in soup factory.

Chapter Three

SOLAR ELECTRIC CATS

There are few solar electric cats in the world today. This is because cats have little use for electricity.

While they do like to sit atop warm television sets and electric blankets, they see little sense in expending the great effort required to produce electricity for heating when they can much more easily get warm by just sitting in the sun.

This is not to say that cats see no value in electricity. They are strongly in favor of maintaining sufficient electric power generating capacity for certain of their needs.[1] However, as long as people kindly supply them with free food and electricity, cats will keep their own power generating capacity in reserve, in case people some day "pull the plug" on their own civilization.

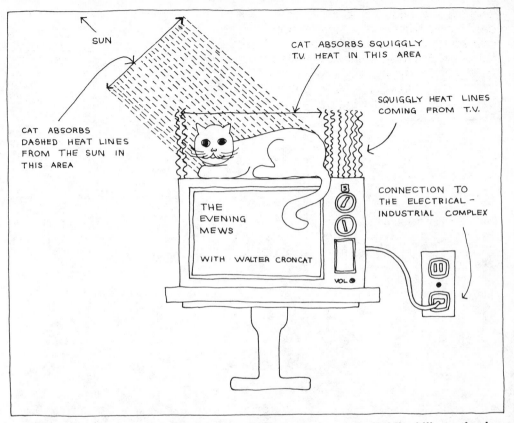

Cat appreciating the existence of electricity, being mindful that it's easier to get warm using direct solar energy.

[1]These include cat food production and cat health care services.

People, of course, can barely conceive of life without electricity. When it was first introduced, they were astonished at its seemingly unlimited potential. Today electricity is as commonplace as background radiation, and is used in virtually every aspect of modern life.

Peoples' great demand for electricity has caused them to study and develop many methods of power generation. Among these are several promising and a few not–so–promising solar electric conversion technologies. The most important of these methods are described in the remainder of this chapter, as well as the method cats chose as the best way to convert sunlight to electricity.

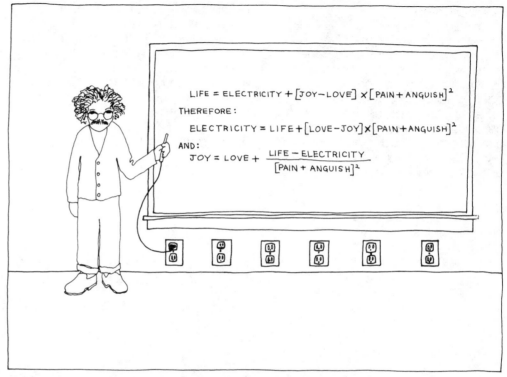

Leading human life-theorist lecturing to post-doctoral class.

$$LIFE = ELECTRICITY + [JOY - LOVE] \times [PAIN + ANGUISH]^2$$

$$THEREFORE:$$

$$ELECTRICITY = LIFE + [LOVE - JOY] \times [PAIN + ANGUISH]^2$$

$$AND:$$

$$JOY = LOVE + \frac{LIFE - ELECTRICITY}{[PAIN + ANGUISH]^2}$$

POWER TOWER
SOLAR ELECTRIC PLANTS

"Power tower" solar electric generating plants have acres of computer controlled mirrors, each of which bounce sunlight onto a small receiver atop a tall central tower. A great amount of sunlight can then be concentrated, producing high enough temperatures to make steam and electricity with conventional turbine generators.

Many think that "power tower" plants require solution of so many difficult technical problems that they bear close resemblance to giant turkeys.

To get around the problems associated with turkeys, the U.S. Department of Energy, in cooperation with the Department of Defense is considering construction of a giant solar cat in the desert near Barstow, California. The proposed $800 billion project would produce a 100 million ton cat which could duplicate a solar cat's basic method for capturing energy.

Government planners hope this cat can be taught to catch Soviet ICBMs as if they were birds, and scoop Russian submarines from the oceans as if they were fish. Other more peaceful applications of the giant cat are also being investigated.

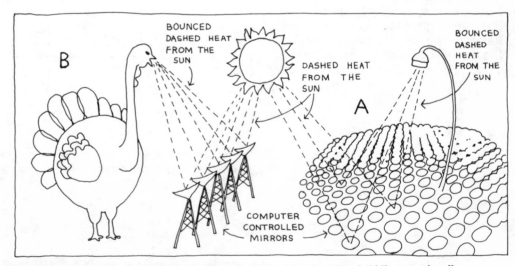

Two kinds of "power tower" solar electric plants: Plant "A" as actually constructed. Plant "B" as viewed by someone not fond of such things.

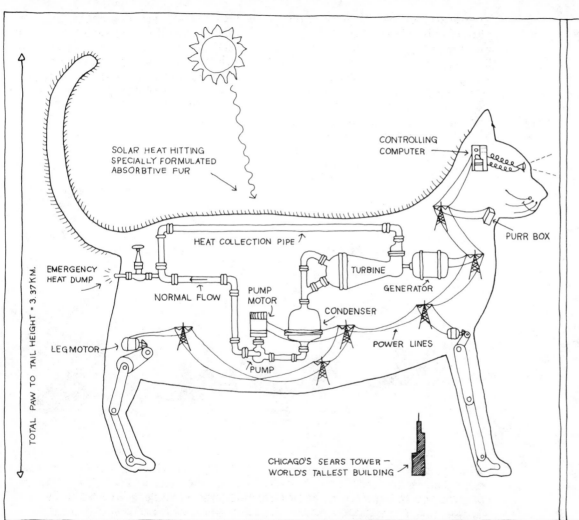

SOLAR HEAT HITTING
SPECIALLY FORMULATED
ABSORBTIVE FUR

CONTROLLING
COMPUTER

PURR BOX

HEAT COLLECTION PIPE

TURBINE

GENERATOR

EMERGENCY
HEAT DUMP

NORMAL FLOW

PUMP
MOTOR

CONDENSER

POWER LINES

LEG MOTOR

PUMP

TOTAL PAW TO TAIL HEIGHT = 3.37 KM.

CHICAGO'S SEARS TOWER —
WORLD'S TALLEST BUILDING

100 MEGATON
DEMONSTRATION
SOLAR CAT

PROPOSED SITE:
BARSTOW, CALIFORNIA

NOTE:
DRAWING DOES NOT SHOW
CONDENSER COOLING LOOP
USING TAIL AS A CLOSED
LOOP, DRY COOLING TOWER

WIND SYSTEMS

Cats usually do not like wind because it messes up their fur and makes it difficult for them to hear birds and approaching dogs. However, they do agree that the wind carries a great deal of energy and would surely harness it if their electrical needs were greater.

People have developed many ways to apply wind energy to their own needs. Windmills were a common part of the American landscape before the massive rural electrification program of the 1930s. Wind systems are again being revived by people who are experimenting with many new types.

Some people are even attempting to incorporate cats in new and exotic wind machines. It is hoped that by using cats, efficiencies can be increased. It is doubtful, however, that more than 60% of the wind's energy can be extracted by any wind machine, with or without cats.

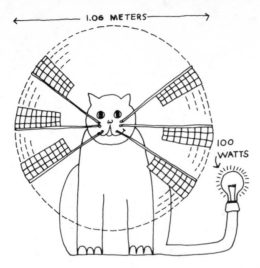

1.06 METERS

100 WATTS

A 60 per cent efficient wind electric catmill as seen by 15 mph wind, illustrating how much power can be extracted from the wind by a cat (or wind) mill of familiar size.

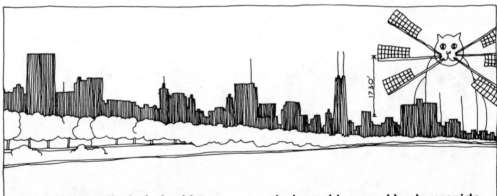

1730'

A 30 million watt wind electric catmill superimposed on the skyline of Chicago to illustrate how large a wind machine must be to provide 30 megawatts in a 10.2 mph wind, the Windy City's mean wind speed.

The most important thing to remember about wind is that its power increases immensely with its speed. For example, a 20 mph wind has eight times as much power as does a 10 mph wind. This means that small wind machines in windy places can produce as much power as much larger machines in less windy places. Sites with the highest average winds will therefore be the first to be commercially developed as "wind power farms."

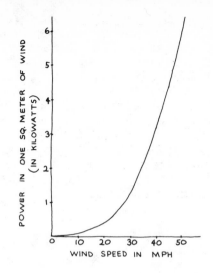

Graph illustrating the great increase in wind power with wind speed.

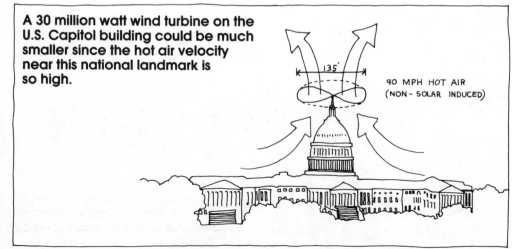

A 30 million watt wind turbine on the U.S. Capitol building could be much smaller since the hot air velocity near this national landmark is so high.

135'

90 MPH HOT AIR
(NON-SOLAR INDUCED)

OCEAN SYSTEMS

Through cats' eyes, the ocean's only saving grace is its supply of tuna and other tasty fish. People, while valuing fish, also see several ways to extract energy from the sea, though none now appear terribly promising.

Ocean Thermal Energy Conversion (OTEC) systems convert the ocean's heat energy into electric power using the temperature difference between surface and deep water. OTEC systems would consist of enormous floating machines using an evaporation-condensation cycle with fluids such as ammonia or freon. The evaporated fluid drives a turbine and electric generator. While OTEC systems have received much more government funding than other ocean systems, they seemed doomed to remain on the drawing board forever, if not only because they are too heavy to lift.

Wave power machines tend to blow away in storms but are otherwise a wonderful idea. They share with OTEC systems the serious problem of transporting electric power to shore.

Machines which harness the energy of ocean tides are being developed but are not practical except in places with wide tidal swings and the proper coastal geography. Since such locations are rare, tidal power is of limited potential.

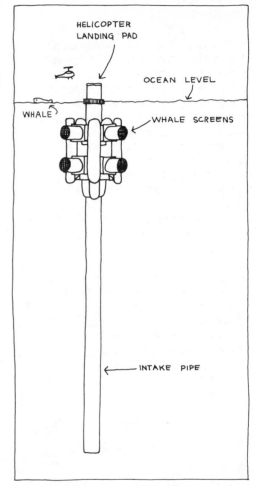

Expected size of a 100 megawatt OTEC plant.

PHOTOVOLTAICS

Photovoltaic cells convert sunlight directly into electricity with only sub-atomic moving parts. Their inner workings can be explained quite simply by imagining that sunlight comes in very small, separate and discrete units called "pho-toms."[1] Each "pho-tom" which hits the surface of the cell completely vanishes upon impact, but leaves behind a tiny "hole" into which nearby electrons fall. The movement of these electrons creates an electric current which is then channeled to an external circuit.

Photovoltaic cells produce "direct" current which must be changed into "alternating" current for most household uses, and like all solar energy conversion methods, they need some means of storage (usually batteries) to deliver power at night.

[1]Scientists are still pondering over the exact nature of light, the concept of "pho-toms" being similar to what they call "photons."

INDIVIDUAL, DISCRETE, PHO-TOMS

ELECTRONS FALLING OR JUMPING INTO VACANT HOLES

PHOTOVOLTAIC CELL SURFACE

Movement of electrons into vacant "holes" causes electric current in photovoltaic cell.

Many people do not like to call photovoltaic cells by their real name. They often simply call them "solar cells" not realizing that a solar cell could be something entirely different.

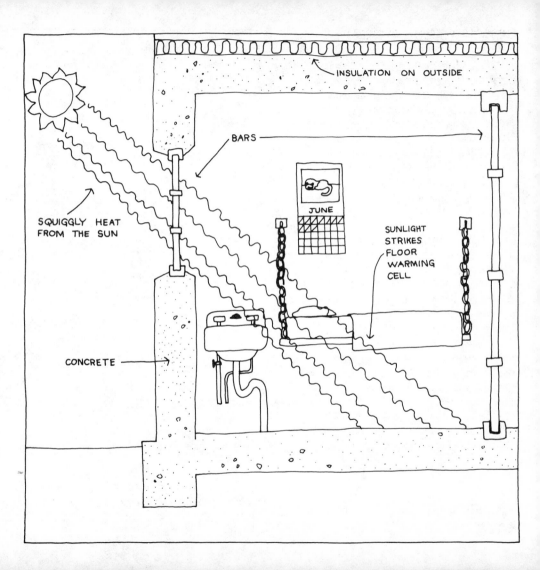

INSULATION ON OUTSIDE

BARS

SQUIGGLY HEAT FROM THE SUN

JUNE

SUNLIGHT STRIKES FLOOR WARMING CELL

CONCRETE

ORBITING SATELLITE SYSTEMS

Another government inspired solar project takes advantage of America's experience in space technology. This time the plan is to place vast fields of photovoltaic cells in orbit whose electrical output would be beamed to earth with microwaves. The estimated cost of this project has reportedly been greatly reduced by using cats in a somewhat unusual way. The revised plan calls for sending 250 million cats into orbit. Scientists expect that the cats will be somewhat unhappy and will meow alot. It is hoped that all that meowing can be directed to the surface of the earth where it would be turned into something more useful.

There is intense debate as to whether or not all that meowing may keep everyone on earth from getting enough sleep. In this sense it seems hardly better than the original proposal which would use extremely powerful and potentially hazardous microwaves for power transmission.

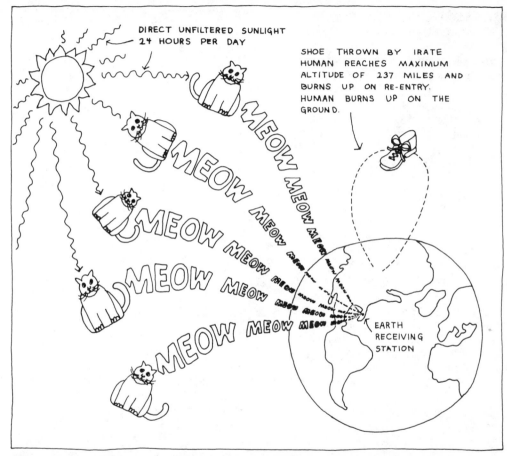

Proposed Federal solar project using meowing cats in permanent orbit which transmit meowing energy to earth. (Note: 5 of 250 million cats shown.)

MEOWIUM DIOXIDE SOLAR ELECTRIC CATS

A meowium dioxide solar electric cat is quite simple in theory yet performs with unfailing reliability. The key to its successful operation is in the meowium dioxide coating which is applied to the cat's fur.

Meowium is a naturally occurring element which people have not yet discovered. Its location on the Periodic Table of the Elements is in a place where human scientists never thought to look. Almost all scientific effort has gone into finding new, heavier elements by throwing smaller elements together in atom smashers and hoping they will stick together. Meowium is found by looking in the other direction, toward things that are so light and fanciful it is a wonder they exist at all! When combined with oxygen to form meowium dioxide (MeO_2) it becomes a very durable coating exhibiting remarkable properties when applied to a cat's fur.

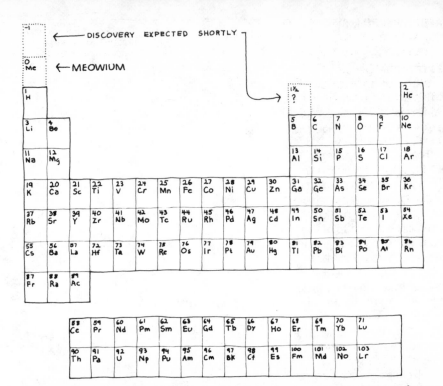

Periodic Table of the Elements showing the location of new elements discovered or about to be discovered by cats. (Note how overall shape of table is moving toward it's ultimate cat-like configuration.)

When meowium dioxide is applied to the fur of a cat with color variations in its coat (such as a tabby cat) an electric voltage is produced between the different colored areas in the presence of sunlight. Electrons move from dark to light fur areas and their movement causes an electric current. In a properly bred solar electric cat, this current can be channeled to charge special portable batteries. The stored power can then be periodically discharged by plugging a special tail adaptor plug into any household outlet. The energy would then be injected into the electric utility's power lines for use elsewhere.

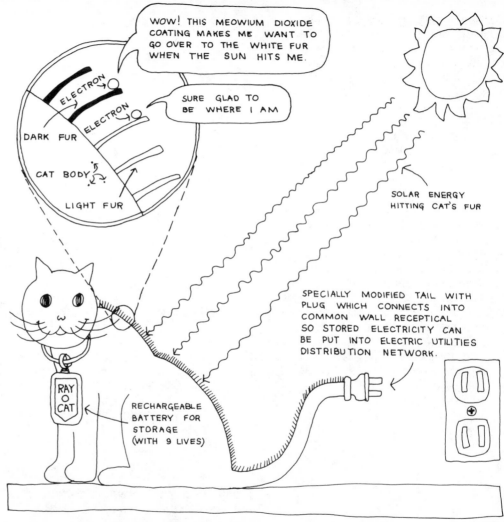

Electricity produced by meowium dioxide solar electric cats is amazingly inexpensive. This is because a little meowium goes a long way and is very cheap to begin with. In addition, solar electric cat systems of this type are generally 90 to 98 per cent efficient! This is in contrast to the most advanced human photovoltaic cells, now struggling to attain 15 per cent conversion of solar energy into electricity.

All this makes solar electric cat systems very attractive to people. Cats realize the value of their solar electric systems but will not allow people in on their central secret: meowium. Cats fear and perhaps rightfully so, that people would stop at nothing to exploit this energy source. The possibility of people raising huge herds of ill fed outdoor cats merely for production of electricity is a thought no responsible cat would allow to come to fruition.

Many unhappy meowium dioxide solar electric cats in desert plugged into the electric utility distribution system.

SOLAR ELECTRIC SUMMARY

Peoples' solar electric conversion technologies are all interesting and expensive.[1] They are so interesting that people often lose sight of the fact that it is still cheaper and much easier to reduce the need to generate more power.

Certainly, one of America's most important tasks is to somehow convince people how to conserve and be more efficient with the electricity they do use. Sophisticated psychological experiments are now being conducted to find the best way of doing this.

[1]Except for hydroelectric power which was ignored in this book since the principles behind this technology are well known.

Chapter Four

SOLAR CAT ECONOMICS

Dr. Milton Friedcat, Emilyville, California, July 29, 1979

Most solar cats are quite economical. In solar lingo, they are quite cost effective.

The noted economist, Dr. Milton Friedcat, has long been a staunch proponent of solar cats. Of course, this is to be expected as Dr. Friedcat is a cat.

The basic task of economics as applied to solar cats is in cost comparison to other forms of energy. The first step in any such comparison is to know the true value of solar energy. Then each method of using it can be better evaluated.

THE VALUE OF SOLAR ENERGY

In order to really appreciate the value of solar energy, it is necessary to understand the difference between energy and power. Energy is the amount of work something can do. Power is how fast the work can be done, or the rate of energy use.[1]

For example, a single government employee can lift a one-pound stack of forms from a desk top to a shelf one foot above desk level in six hours. If 21,600 identically capable civil servants could somehow work in unison (with no loss of efficiency) to accomplish the same task, only one second would be required. The same amount of energy was expended in each case, however the multitude of paper lifters applied much more power to the same task.

[1]This says nothing of how efficiently the energy is applied to the task. Also, according to this definition, the U.S. and other industrial nations are experiencing a power crisis, not an energy crisis, which may be why everyone is so confused.

In the world of metric units, a kilowatt is a measure of power, and a kilowatt-hour is a measure or distinct quantity of energy. A kilowatt-hour of electricity now costs about ten cents in many places, while kilowatt-hours of gasoline cost about three cents each.

In order to appreciate how much power (and energy) is in sunlight, the concept of a "metric cat" is helpful. About one kilowatt of solar power falls on a metric cat whose one square meter absorbing area is oriented perpendicular to the sun's rays in bright sunlight. In one hour, one kilowatt-hour of solar energy would hit that cat.

In most places, a rate of one kilowatt per square meter occurs only during the middle of the day. The rate at which solar energy hits anything is less in the morning and afternoon, and is much much less at night. Weather also has a lot to do with how much sun can hit a cat.

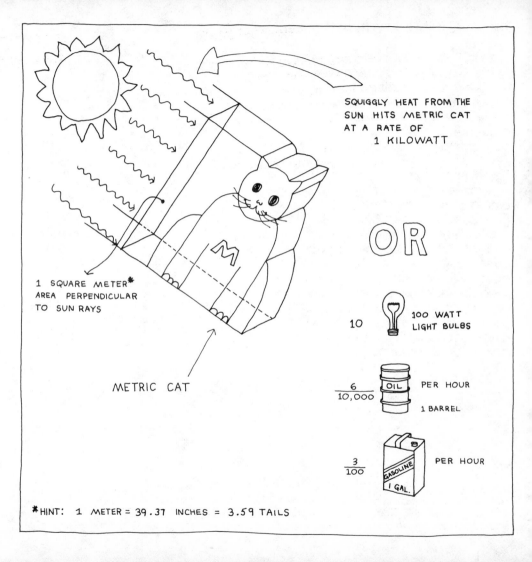

SQUIGGLY HEAT FROM THE SUN HITS METRIC CAT AT A RATE OF 1 KILOWATT

OR

10 · 100 WATT LIGHT BULBS

$\frac{6}{10,000}$ OIL · PER HOUR · 1 BARREL

$\frac{3}{100}$ GASOLINE 1 GAL. · PER HOUR

1 SQUARE METER* AREA PERPENDICULAR TO SUN RAYS

METRIC CAT

*HINT: 1 METER = 39.37 INCHES = 3.59 TAILS

It is useful to know how much solar energy will hit a particular surface over a much longer period, so that short term variations are averaged out.

About 1,700 kilowatt-hours of solar energy fall on a typical, horizontal square meter of absolutely average America each year. If this much energy was converted entirely into gasoline, (as with horizontal metric gas cats) enough gas would be produced to fuel a 30 mpg car 1,364 miles. An average American car owner would merely need several such cats in order to stay happily rolling along.

Of course, no one lives in an absolutely average American place. Also, no one has yet perfected a 100% efficient metric gas cat! Nonetheless, even people in such cloudy places as Seattle would need only about 1½ times as many metric gas cats to make the same amount of gas.

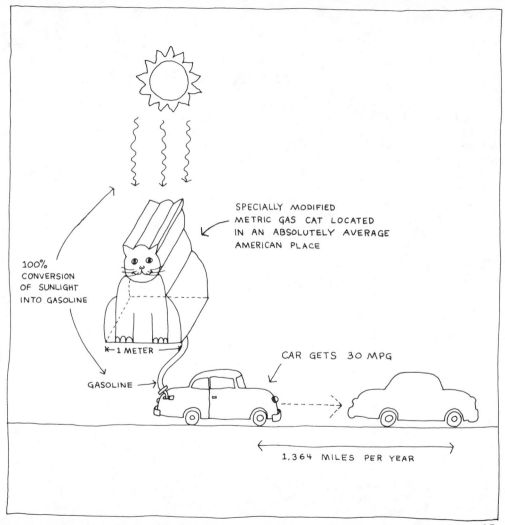

SPECIALLY MODIFIED METRIC GAS CAT LOCATED IN AN ABSOLUTELY AVERAGE AMERICAN PLACE

100% CONVERSION OF SUNLIGHT INTO GASOLINE

← 1 METER

GASOLINE →

CAR GETS 30 MPG

1,364 MILES PER YEAR

SOLAR THERMAL CAT ECONOMICS

As discussed earlier, two kinds of solar thermal cats are of practical interest: "passive" cats and "active" cats. With both kinds, initial purchase and installation costs are very small. Operating and maintenance costs are modest for each kind, with passive cats costing less for veterinary care and food.[1]

Peoples' solar thermal systems are not nearly as economical as solar cats, but they do pretty well nonetheless. In comparison, peoples' systems usually have high first costs, low operating and maintenance costs, and produce modest amounts of energy. As with cats, peoples' passive solar thermal systems do somewhat better than the active kind.

[1]Detailed economic calculations for an active solar cat system, of the type pictured on the cover of this book, appear in the Appendix.

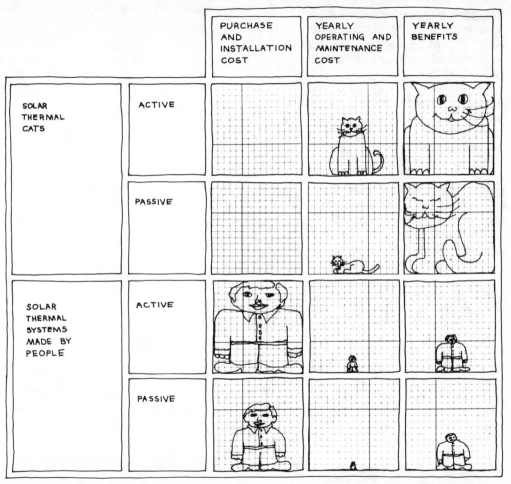

Cost-benefit comparison chart. (Note: the bigger the figure, the bigger the cost or benefit.)

Since the benefits of solar cats so greatly outweigh the costs, they are obviously good investments. Peoples' solar systems take longer before their benefits equal and surpass the initial costs. The time it takes for this to occur is called the "payback time," and is easy to figure out by dividing the purchase and installation costs by the yearly benefits minus the yearly operating and maintenance costs.

Many years ago, economists invented inflation as a way to achieve job security. Inflation makes everything more complicated, and causes a great demand for ever more professional economists. Inflation however, makes solar thermal systems look even more attractive, because the benefit of solar system operation (fuel cost savings) inflates faster than everything else! Solar thermal cats (and actually peoples' systems as well) are therefore an excellent hedge against inflation.

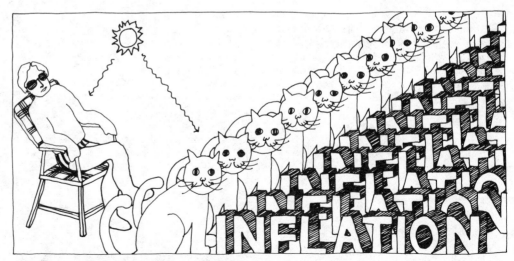

Solar cats as a hedge against inflation.

The biggest problem with peoples' solar thermal systems is that they cost a lot to buy and install. Today, an average active solar water heating system costs $2,500. The largest costs are for the collector and installation labor.

Many people expect costs of solar systems to decrease as new and cheaper collectors are devised. However, the cost of the collectors are less than half the cost of the whole system, and cost reductions that do occur are not likely to offset inflation.

Significant cost reductions are far more likely for photovoltaic cells as discussed later.

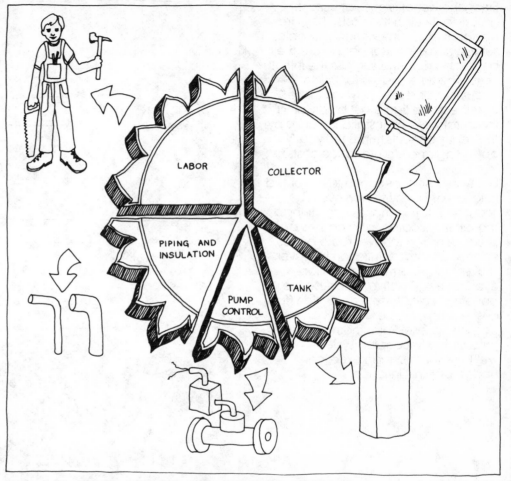

First cost breakdown for a typical active solar domestic water heating system.

SOLAR ELECTRIC CAT ECONOMICS

Little is known of the economics of meowium dioxide solar electric cats (see Chapter Three), since cats won't talk to people about meowium, and leave few recorded messages. Until people discover how to obtain meowium, any talk about the economics of these systems is pure conjecture. Professional conjecturists (commonly known as economists) suspect that electricity produced by this method "will be too cheap to meter." Only time will tell if they are correct.

Of peoples' methods for solar electric conversion, only hydroelectric power is currently cheap enough to produce on a large scale. The other methods described in Chapter Three are really just beginning the race toward economic feasibility. Though meowium dioxide solar electric cats have probably already won, it will be interesting to see who comes in second.

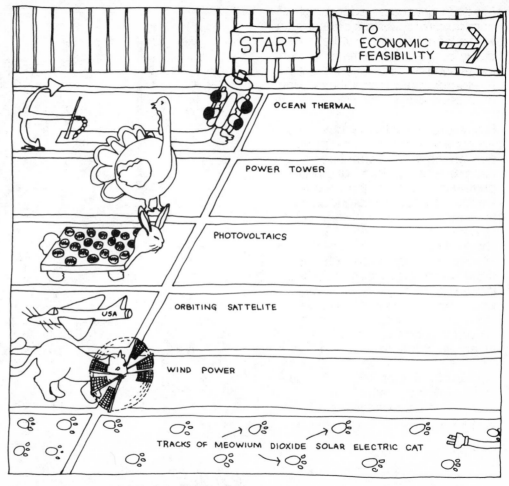

The race to economic feasibility.

Although great cost reductions have occurred, photovoltaic cells remain very expensive. An intense effort is being made to further reduce costs to the $500 per kilowatt range, considered by many a realistic, attainable goal.

Even then, added costs for storage of excess energy and for equipment to convert the direct current cell output into properly regulated alternating current may prevent their ever becoming economically feasible for general household use.

They will however, find increasing use in a wide variety of somewhat specialized applications. These will include providing power for recharging small, portable devices like flashlights, radios, and tape recorders, and for general use in remote locations.

Perhaps the largest eventual market for photovoltaic cells will be in recharging the batteries of tomorrow's electric cars.

INCOME CATS CREDITS

One of the ways that the government has chosen to hasten the development and use of solar energy systems is with <u>income tax credits</u>. When a solar system is installed on the residence of an income tax payer, a percentage of the cost of the system can be claimed as a direct personal income tax credit. This serves to reduce the first cost of solar systems making their payback times shorter.

No such tax credit yet exists for solar cats, since their first costs are already quite low. However, a similar credit on veterinary bills and cat food costs has been proposed for each cat that comes into a home. Such an <u>income cats credit</u> would pay for all operating and maintenance costs of the cat in question, as long as it was counted.

One drawback of this proposal is the need to form yet another government bureaucracy in order to count cats.

Employee of U.S. Income Cats Counting Bureau at work.

Chapter Five

HOW TO CHOOSE A SOLAR CAT

There are many ways to select a solar cat. However, choosing a good one is not easy, as countless variables complicate a clear choice. The same problem arises when people try to choose solar heating systems. In either case, it is best to look at each part of the cat or system and, using common sense, see if it seems adequate in view of what it is supposed to do.

If common sense doesn't work, there are always experts to help out. Experts on any subject are always nearby, but choosing an expert is equally difficult, and should certainly not be left to blind chance.

Person selecting a solar cat.

Person selecting an expert.

There are many good books which tell about things to consider when selecting a human-designed solar thermal system. A few of these books are listed in the Appendix. In addition to reading, a good way to find out about a particular system is to talk to someone who has owned and operated one for a few years. In this way, the selection process becomes very similar to that of buying a new car.

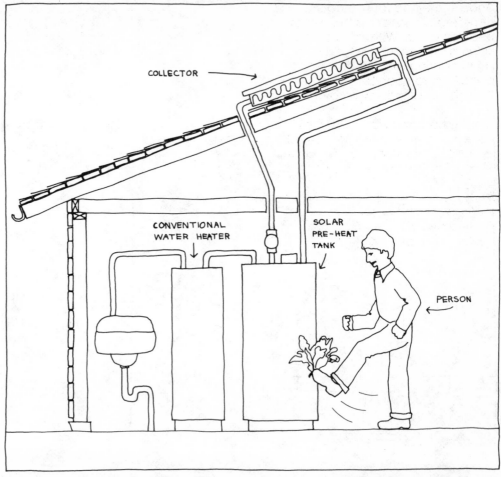

COLLECTOR

CONVENTIONAL WATER HEATER

SOLAR PRE-HEAT TANK

PERSON

Person evaluating a solar water heating system using automotive technique.

Another method for evaluating and choosing a solar cat is the 10 day free home trial. With this method, a kitten is brought home for a 10 day period during which the prospective owners get a chance to examine it in the privacy of their own home.[1]

This method also works well for kittens in search of a home as few people are able to resist falling into "kitty-love" after about one week.[2]

An interesting aspect of this selection method is that it really forces the prospective owners to examine their reasons for wanting a cat in the first place.

[1]Some "free" trial offers do not include kitty litter, litter box, kitty food, food and water dishes, flea soap or kitty toys, and are therefore not as free as they could be.

[2]Kitty love is similar to puppy love, but is softer, yet more serious.

HARRY I'M STILL NOT SURE IT GOES WELL WITH THE DRAPES. MAYBE IT WOULD LOOK BETTER IN CHARTREUSE?

THE SOLAR CAT EVALUATION CHECKLIST

Many people do not have the time to read books, to choose (or listen to) experts, to embark on 10 day free home trials, or to think for themselves. The Solar Cat Evaluation Checklist is made especially for these people. It is particularly useful in comparing two or more cats, although it does attempt to set absolute standards for goodness from "very bad" to "very very good."[1]

To use the checklist, carefully determine the correct rating for each evaluation item for the cat under consideration. Then determine the Solar Cat Evaluation Number and Evaluation Rating Classification.

If a great many cats are to be evaluated, the "SOLCAT" computer program may be of value. The SOLCAT program is explained, and a program listing is presented in the Appendix.

[1]There is one category for cats better than "very very good," but few cats ever attain such a rating.

STANDARD SOLAR CAT EVALUATION CHECKLIST

Evaluation Item	Rating (1 to 10 or as indicated)
A. Is it really a cat? (10 is very much a cat)	_____
B. Number of paws (insert actual number of paws)	_____
C. Width of left front paw (in inches)	_____
D. Length of tail (in paws)	_____
E. Maximum cross sectional area (in square paws)	_____
F. Weight of cat (undressed and dry)	_____
G. Fur color (black = 10, white = 1, transparent = 0)	_____
H. Number of stripes (if no stripes, enter 0)	_____
I. Width of stripes (in paws, if no stripes, enter 0)	_____
J. Number of fur colors	_____
K. Maximum purr rate (in purrs per minute)	_____
L. Average fur length (in paws)	_____
M. Fear of dogs	_____
N. How much it likes to eat	_____
O. How much it likes to lie in the sun	_____

To determine the Solar Cat Evaluation Number (SCEN), insert the checklist rating values into the following equation and add, multiply or divide as appropriate:

$$SCEN = A \times E \times F \times G \times O \times [B + C + D + H + I + J + K + L + \frac{1}{M+1} + N]$$

There are several ways to interpret the result of this equation. One way is to consider it nonsense and get the cat you like the most. This method is considered quite reliable. But for those who don't know what they like, it is generally considered that high values of "SCEN" are best, and low or negative values are not so good. If you come up with imaginary numbers (and there really are such things), you have great potential as a solar cat owner, but not as a mathematician. It is certainly easy to compare the SCENs of two cats under review, the cat with the higher SCEN being the better bet.

If only one cat is under review, its SCEN can be compared to the Standard Solar Cat Evaluation Rating Classifications as presented in the following table:

TABLE OF STANDARD SOLAR CAT EVALUATION RATING CLASSIFICATIONS

SCEN	Evaluation Rating Classification
0 and below	very bad
above 0, up to 10,000	not so bad, not so good
above 10,000 up to 1,000,000	fair
above 1,000,000 up to 10,000,000	pretty good
above 10,000,000 up to 100,000,000	very good
above 100,000,000 up to 1,000,000,000	very very good
above 1,000,000,000	Unbelievable! (but not unique)

Chapter Six

OPERATING, TRAINING, AND MAINTAINING A SOLAR CAT

The key to long lasting, efficient solar cat operation is in effective operation, training, and maintenance. This chapter presents important concepts in formulating an effective program to accomplish this, as cats seldom come with their own instructions.[1]

OPERATION

Cats are fully automatic and need little or no input from anyone in order to function efficiently. However, they can break down and it is advisable to become familiar with how cats work so that substandard performance is quickly identified and corrected. Learning about cats can be accomplished by reading books about cats, and by going to classes, seminars and lectures about cats. Direct observation of cats "in the field" is also of great value, there being no academic substitute for practical experience.

Engaging the services of a professional cat repair specialist.

Substandard solar cat performance can occur either because the cat forgot what it was supposed to do or it got sick, hurt, or otherwise damaged. If the problem can be traced to amnesia, a cat training program is in order. If the cat is sick, hurt or damaged, the services of a professional cat repair specialist should be sought.

[1]Programs in which Training precedes Operation and Maintenance are commonly called "T.O.M. Cat" programs.

TRAINING

Contrary to popular belief, it is possible to train a cat! Historically, the greatest success has been in training them to do things they were about to do anyway. However, limited success has been reported in other areas.

Cats learn some things very quickly, such as how to purr, where and when cat food appears, or how to proceed (or recede) as menacing dogs approach. Other things are much more difficult for them to pick up, such as how to drive trucks or become successful prizefighters.

Cat being trained how to purr (successfully).

Man in cat suit jumping rope trying (unsuccessfully) to get cat to do the same.

79

If a cat does not like to sit in the sun to absorb energy, it is sometimes possible to bring the sun to the cat, either with mirrors, or clever cat food dish location.[1] If such devious methods do not work, more effort should be devoted to proper cat selection (see Chapter Five).

Cat having more important things to do than to lie in the sun.

Cat absorbing sunlight while eating.

[1]Never keep cat food in the sun, as it will spoil quickly. It is the cat you want to sit in the sun, not the cat food!

MAINTENANCE

Proper maintenance of solar cats is best accomplished with strict adherence to a properly formulated maintenance schedule. Since each cat has different servicing needs, no single maintenance schedule applies in all cases. The sample schedule presented here should therefore be reviewed and modified as necessary by a professional cat maintenance specialist, in view of the cat under consideration.

(1) A purrometer can be used to count purrs
(2) If necessary
(3) General external inspection for appearance, attitude, and appetite.
(4) Inspect cat's stool (and urine if possible) for abnormalities.
(5) Applies only to cats who are allowed outside.
(6) Applies only to cats who have removable and interchangeable paws.
(7) Inspection and servicing by a professional cat maintenance service.

(SAMPLE) SOLAR CAT MAINTENANCE SCHEDULE

SERVICE INTERVAL	ITEM	REMOVE	TELL	LOVE	C.F.L.*	REFILL	CLEAN	INSPECT	SERVICE
12 Hours or 12,000 Purrs[1] (Whichever occurs first)	Cat			X					
	Water Dish				X	(2)			
	Food Dish					X	X	X	
24 Hours or 24,000 Purrs (Whichever occurs first)	Cat			X				(3)	
	Water Dish					X	X		
	Food Dish					X	X		
	Litter Box						X	(4)	
	Mouse toes in bed	X						X	
	Bird feathers	X						X	
	Fur						X	X	
Every second Litter Box change	Go outside, cat! (5)		X						
	Paw rotation (6)								X
7 days or 168,000 Purrs (Whichever occurs first)	Ears							X	(2)
	Teeth							X	(2)
	Fleas	X							
1 Month or 720,000 Purrs (Whichever occurs first)	Cat			X			X	X	X
1 year or 8.76 Megapurrs (Whichever occurs first)	Cat							(7)	(7)

*CHECK FLUID LEVEL

Conclusion

Cats know a good thing when they see one, be it a fresh, juicy fish, or a clean, efficient energy source. People are equally perceptive regarding fish, but have trouble recognizing good energy options.

Laughter helps to clear one's mind, and often allows clever insights to emerge. So if this book made you smile, it accomplished its basic purpose. Even if you didn't find it funny you may have learned something about solar energy, which is certainly good—nearly as good as cats.

ACTIVE SOLAR THERMAL CAT ECONOMIC CALCULATIONS

The following calculations apply to an active solar thermal cat system of the kind pictured on the cover of this book.

Please note that throughout these calculations, costs are expressed in terms of 1979 U.S. dollars.

1. A standard cat (see Appendix, Part Three) whose body temperature is 100.5°F goes outside to warm up in the sun. (Note: the normal body temperature of a cat can range from 100.5°F to 102.0°F and can vary throughout a day.)

2. The sun hits each square foot of the cat's fur at a rate of 300 BTU per hour (a common mid-day rate).

3. The cat fur is especially absorptive and collects 90% of the solar energy that hits it.

   This results in:

$$300 \times 0.90 = 270 \text{ BTU absorbed per hour per square foot of cat fur}$$

4. The total area of cat fur exposed to sunlight in a plane perpendicular to the rays of the sun is 192 square inches, or 1.33 square feet, so that:

   $$\begin{array}{r} 270.0 \\ \times 1.33 \\ \hline 359.1 \end{array}$$

   270.0 BTU per hour absorbed per square foot of cat
   × 1.33 square feet of cat fur per cat
   359.1 BTU per hour absorbed per cat

5. The cat can absorb solar energy until its body temperature reaches 102.0°F at which time the cat returns indoors to discharge the collected energy to the interior of the house. Since it starts out at 100.5°F, its temperature has increased 1.5°F, and in so doing it absorbs 15 BTUs. At a rate of 359.1 BTU per hour it will take 2.51 minutes to heat the cat from 100.5 to 102.0°F, since:

$$\frac{15 \text{ BTU per cat} \times 60 \text{ min. per hour}}{359.1 \text{ BTU per hour per cat}} = 2.51 \text{ minutes}$$

6. If we assume that the cat takes 3 minutes for its outdoor trip, and 7 minutes to discharge the heat to interior of the house, 10 minutes are required to complete each round trip cycle.

7. When inside, the cat discharges both the stored solar heat collected in its body of 15 BTU, and the catabolic heat generated by normal cat body functioning.

The catabolic heat generation rate can be estimated from the equation presented in the section on catabolism in Chapter Two which predicts a 92.8 BTU per hour catabolic heat generation rate for the standard 10 lb. cat. Since the cat spends 7 minutes indoors discharging heat, the total catabolic heat put into the house is:

$$\frac{7 \text{ minutes}}{60 \text{ min. per hour}} \times 92.8 \text{ BTU per hour} = 10.8 \text{ BTU}$$

When the solar heat input of 15 BTU is added:

$$10.8 + 15 = 25.8 \text{ BTU}$$

is put into the house during each complete charge and discharge cycle.

8. Since each cycle is 10 minutes long, 6 cycles can be completed each hour. If an average of 8 hours of cycling can occur each day of a 250 day heating season, the yearly heat input to the house as a result of this cycling is as follows:

6 cycles/hr. × 8 hours/day = 48 cycles/day

48 cycles/day × 250 days/yr. = 12000 cycles/yr.

12000 cycles/yr. × 25.8 BTU/cycle = 309,600 BTU/yr.

9. Since the cat is on its "solar cycle" only 8 hours per day, the remaining 16 hours per day can be spent hanging around inside the house discharging catabolic heat at a rate of 92.8 BTUs per hour, so that:

92.8 BTU/hour × 16 hours/day = 1484.8 BTU/day

is input to the house by night time catabolic heat generation. In a 250 day season, this comes to:

1484.8 BTU/day × 250 days/year = 371,200 BTU/year

10. If we now add the daytime and nightime heat inputs:

309,600 BTU per year (Daytime)
371,200 BTU per year (Nightime)
680,800 BTU per year

is supplied to the house by the solar cat.

11. If this energy was supplied instead by electric resistance heating, at a cost of $0.10 per kilowatt hour, the value of the solar cat energy would be $19.95 per year. While $19.95 per year per cat is nothing to sneeze at, normal operating and maintenance costs certainly are! These include food, flea collar, and veterinary costs as follows:

A. Flea collars

$3.98/collar × 3 collars/year = $11.94/year/cat

B. Food

> 0.5 cans of wet food per day per cat
> at $0.30 per can yields $0.15 per day per cat

> 50 grams of dry food per day per cat
> at $0.0012 per gram yields $0.06 per day per cat

Therefore, the total yearly cat food cost is:

$$\$0.15 + \$0.06 = \$0.21 \times 365 = \$76.65$$

C. Veterinary care

These costs vary from zero to several hundred dollars per year. As no widely accepted (or even proposed) average number for such costs exists, the average yearly veterinary costs for a typical standard active solar thermal cat are hereby:

$$\$110.91 \text{ per year per cat}$$

The total operating and maintenance costs are then:

$ 11.94	for fleas protection
76.65	for cat food
+ 110.91	for veterinary care
$199.50	Total operating and maintenance costs per year per cat

12. Operating and maintenance costs are therefore ten times the yearly savings! This obviously will not do, if solar cats are to be really feasible!

Several things can be done to make the picture look a whole lot better:

A. Use "passive" cats to reduce veterinary and food costs. Passive cats also add more catabolic heat since they seldom go outside. (The fact that they also don't bring in any heat from outside can be conveniently ignored.)

B. Consider additional energy input due to "latent purrs," as explained in Chapter Two. This item alone could increase the output of a sufficiently happy solar cat by a factor of 100 or more!

C. Pass the federal income cats credit as described in Chapter Four, thereby eliminating all direct costs to the cat owner, while spreading them out over all of society.

D. Let them eat cake! This famous European solution would effectively eliminate food costs.

THE "SOLCAT" SOLAR CAT EVALUATION COMPUTER PROGRAM

The "SOLCAT" computer program was first written on a Data General model S-130 minicomputer in their version of the "BASIC" computer language. Other computers may have slightly different versions of the "BASIC" language, so the program listing as presented here might not work properly at first try.

The SOLCAT program goes through the same, simple checklist and evaluation procedure which appears in Chapter Five. Though an average eighth grade student (with pencil) could easily use the "long hand" checklist method, the "SOLCAT" program allows one to use the latest in sophisticated electronic technology to accomplish the same task!

"SOLCAT" PROGRAM LISTING

```
0005  DIM V$(40), Z$ (25)
0006  PRINT
0007  PRINT
0010  PRINT  "Welcome to SOLCAT—Version 1.0"
0020  PRINT
0030  PRINT  "This program aids in selecting a solar cat."
0040  PRINT  "Answer the following questions about the cat"
0050  PRINT  "under evaluation. After answering all questions"
0060  PRINT  "the program will automatically tell you how good"
0070  PRINT  "or bad the cat is. It then allows you to start"
0080  PRINT  "all over again in case you want to get a"
0090  PRINT  "different answer, or have another cat to"
0100  PRINT  "evaluate."
0105  PRINT
```

```
0110 PRINT
0120 PRINT "All questions should be answered with a number"
0130 PRINT "from 1 to 10 unless otherwise indicated."
0140 PRINT
0150 PRINT
1000 INPUT "Name of cat (spell it out)                              =",V$
1001 PRINT
1002 INPUT "Is it really a cat? (10 is very much a cat)             =",A
1010 INPUT "Number of paws                                         =",B
1020 INPUT "Width of left front paw (in inches)                    =",C
1030 INPUT "Length of tail (in paws)                               =",D
1040 INPUT "Maximum cross sectional area (in square paws)  =",E
1050 INPUT "Weight of cat (in pounds, undressed and dry)   =",F
1060 INPUT "Fur color (black = 10, white = 1, transparent = 0)  =",G
1070 INPUT "Number of stripes (if no stripes, use 1)               =",H
1080 INPUT "Width of stripes (in paws)                             =",I
1090 INPUT "Number of fur colors                                   =",J
1100 INPUT "Maximum purr rate (in purrs per minute)         =",K
1110 INPUT "Average fur length (in paws)                           =",L
1120 INPUT "Fear of dogs                                           =",M
1130 INPUT "How much it likes to eat                               =",N
1140 INPUT "How much it likes to lie in the sun                    =",O
1150 Q7=0
1200 PRINT
```

```
1220  PRINT
2010  S1 = A*E*F*G*O*(B+C+D+H+I+J+K+L+(1/(1+M))+N)
3000  IF S1 = 0 THEN Z$ = "VERY BAD"
3010  IF S1 < 0 THEN Z$ = "VERY BAD"
3020  IF S1 > 0 THEN GOTO 5000
3100  PRINT USING "SOLAR CAT EVALUATION NO = ###,###,###,###,###,###.##",S1
3110  PRINT
3120  PRINT "SOLAR CAT STANDARD RATING = ",Z$
3124  IF Q7 = 0 THEN GOTO 3130
3125  PRINT
3126  PRINT "Unbelievable! (but not unique)"
3127  PRINT
3128  PRINT "Nevertheless, GET IT QUICK"
3130  PRINT
3150  INPUT "Do you want to start over again? (Y or N)",Y$
3155  PRINT
3156  PRINT
3157  PRINT
3160  IF Y$ = "Y" THEN GOTO 1000
3170  IF Y$ = "y" THEN GOTO 1000
3180  IF Y$ = "YES" THEN GOTO 1000
3190  IF Y$ = "yes" THEN GOTO 1000
3200  IF Y$ = "Yes" THEN GOTO 1000
3210  GOTO 9999
```

```
5000  IF S1 = 10000 THEN GOTO 6000
5010  IF S1 < 10000 THEN GOTO 6000
5020  IF S1 = 1000000 THEN GOTO 6100
5030  IF S1 < 1000000 THEN GOTO 6100
5040  IF S1 = 10000000 THEN GOTO 6200
5050  IF S1 < 10000000 THEN GOTO 6200
5060  IF S1 = 100000000 THEN GOTO 6300
5070  IF S1 < 100000000 THEN GOTO 6300
5080  IF S1 = 1000000000 THEN GOTO 6400
5085  IF S1 < 1000000000 THEN GOTO 6400
5090  GOTO 6500
6000  Z$ = "NOT SO BAD, NOT SO GOOD"
6010  GOTO 3100
6100  Z$ = "FAIR"
6110  GOTO 3100
6200  Z$ = "PRETTY GOOD"
6210  GOTO 3100
6300  Z$ = "VERY GOOD"
6310  GOTO 3100
6400  Z$ = "VERY VERY GOOD"
6410  GOTO 3100
6500  Q7 = 1
6520  GOTO 3100
9999  END
```

CAT THERMAL UNITS (CTUs) AND HEAT

Like the "BTU" or British Thermal Unit, the CTU is a measure of heat energy.[1] However, the CTU is a bit more than just energy.

Both the CTU and BTU are precisely defined amounts of heat. A BTU is commonly defined as enough heat to raise the temperature of one pound of water one degree fahrenheit.[2] There are two kinds of CTUs: small CTUs and big CTUs. A small CTU is exactly enough heat to raise the temperature of the standard cat one degree fahrenheit. The standard cat weighs ten pounds, is gray, has short hair, and is very good. Since cats are comprised primarily of cat food and water, one small CTU is about the same as 10 BTUs.

A big CTU is the amount of heat produced as a result of normal body catabolism of the standard cat over all of its nine lives, assuming that the cat is always at rest, and lives 15 years in each life. Catabolism is discussed in Chapter Two, and is the part of body metabolism in which heat is released. There are 10,980,200 little CTUs in a big CTU. One big CTU also equals about 19.6 barrels of crude oil.

[1]Cats invented the CTU long before anyone invented the British.
[2]There are actually several kinds of BTUs, the International Steam Table (IST) BTU is 4.1868 IST calories, and the Mean BTU is 4.19002 mean calories. CTUs are not mean, so the IST conversion applies.

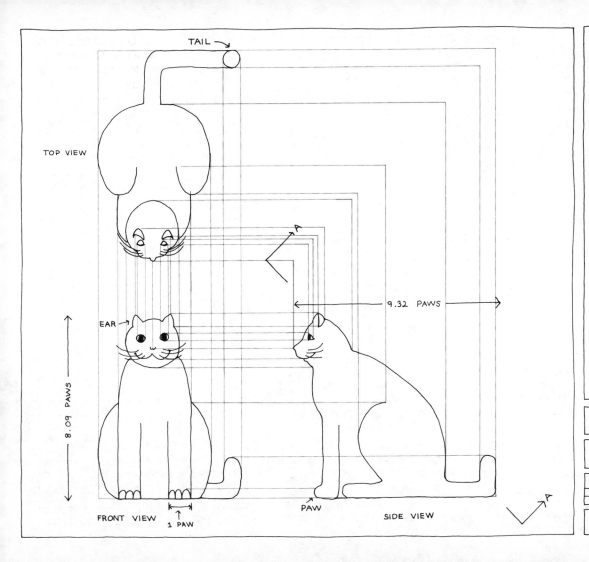

TOP VIEW

TAIL

EAR

FRONT VIEW

1 PAW

PAW

SIDE VIEW

8.09 PAWS

9.32 PAWS

A

A

THE STANDARD CAT

NOTES:

1. GROSS WEIGHT = 10 LBS.
2. FUR COLOR = GRAY
3. NO. OF PAWS = 4.0
4. 1 PAW = 1.37 INCHES
5. 8 PAWS = 1 TAIL
6. TAIL WAGS WHEN ANGRY
7. FUR LENGTH = 0.8 PAWS
8. STOMACH SIZE = UNMEASURABLE
9. MAXIMUM PURR RATE : 173 P.P.M.
   (PURRS PER MINUTE)
10. CROSS-SECTION AREA FACING
    SUN (SECTION A-A) = 96
    SQUARE PAWS

SCALE: NONE (ALL FUR)

BY: M. AUGUSTYN

APPROVALS

CRP.	BAW	J.B.	SYS.
WEM.	CSS.	H3	M

REVISION 0

One very important thing to under-stand about CTUs is that they are very anti-social. They do not like each other at all, and whenever they can, they try to go anyplace where there are fewer CTUs. You can always tell how many CTUs are in something by measuring its temperature. The higher its temperature, the more CTUs are in-side the material in question.

The sun is so grossly overpopulated with CTUs, that in order to get away, solar CTUs literally turn themselves in-to electromagnetic radiation and zoom out from the surface of the sun at the speed of light in all directions. Even if they end up in such a rela-tively cool place as on a cat's fur in the living room of a suburban Ameri-can home, they are not satisfied. They still keep trying to get away from the nearby, though less numerous CTU population. CTUs are not com-pletely happy until they reach the lonely depths of outer space where they can float alone without another CTU within millions of miles.

It is important to note that it is quite easy to hold onto CTUs if there aren't many of them around. The more CTUs there are, the harder it is to keep them in one place, as their dis-taste for each other grows with their

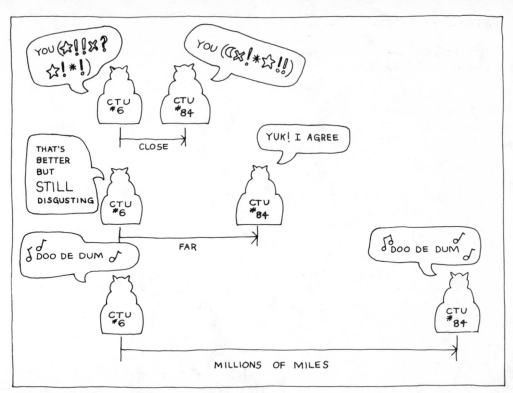

CTU disposition as a function of distance.

numbers. This explains why it is so much easier to keep a house cold on a cold day than it is to keep it warm. When cats or people think about how to keep warm or cool, they are really thinking about how to get and keep the right number of CTUs nearby. Thus, the entire cat and human fields of thermodynamics and heat transfer are devoted to describ-ing precisely how anti-social CTUs (and BTUs) are.

CONCRETE CATS—
THE ALLERGIC SOLUTION

Many people are allergic to cats. To such people, the thought of dozens of furry little electric, active or passive cats running all over the house is disquieting at best.

Solid concrete cats offer a remarkably good solution to this problem, as few peple are allergic to concrete. Concrete cats can be painted dark colors and placed on south facing windowsills to warm up during the day, then carried off to bed to keep sleepers warm at night.

RECOMMENDED READING MATERIAL

1. "The Well Cat Book,"
   by Terri McGinnis, D.V.M., Random House/Bookworks,
   1975, 279 pages

2. "Direct Use of the Sun's Energy,"
   by Farrington Daniels, Ballantine Books, 1964, 271 pages

3. "Solar for Your Present Home,"
   by C. Barnaby, et al., California Energy Commission,
   1978, 163 pages

4. "The Solar Home Book,"
   by Bruce Anderson and Michael Riordan,
   Cheshire Books, 1976, 297 pages

5. "The Passive Solar Energy Book,"
   by Edward Mazria, Rodale Press, 1979, 435 pages

6. "Solar Age,"
   (a magazine), P.O. Box 4934, Manchester, N.H. 03108

7. "Scientific American,"
   (magazine), May 1979 edition, page 130, "A Brain
   Cooling System in Mammals," by Mary Ann Baker

8. "The Fat Cat, A Danish Folktale,"
   by Jack Kent, Scholastic Book Services, March 1973,
   28 pages

Glossary

Advocat—A cat mathematician specializing in addition.

Bad—A cat who is not good.

Cat—The next best thing to the best thing there is.

Catabolism—The part of metabolism in which heat is released: "destructive" metabolism.

Catacomb—A special cat door which arranges cat fur in a desirable manner.

Catta Tonic—Something good to drink.

Conservation—No meaning.

Energy—Everything that isn't mass.

Gasoline—See Sex.

Glop—In liquid form, an anti-corrosive additive to be mixed with potentially corrosive fluids. (In solid form see Yuk.)

Good—Most cats and many people.

Inflation—An imaginary condition in which peoples' energy and work becomes worth less as time goes by.

Kitty—A small cat.

Love—An essential ingredient in any successful solar cat.

Kitty Love—Like puppy love, yet softer and more serious.

Meow—Short for just about anything.

Money—Energy as well as everything that isn't energy.

Oil—See Gasoline.

Politician—See Conservation.

Purr—A form of latent energy storage used by cats having a value defined by depth and frequency.

PPM—Abbreviation for "purrs per minute."

Purrometer—A device used to count purrs consisting of an otherwise unemployed person with stopwatch.

Sex—The opiate of the masses. (See Gasoline.)

Sun—That which turns night into day.

Yuk—Solid glop.